GRIEF TO GLORY:
You Do Not Have to be the STRONG ONE.

Conversation Between Me, Grief, and Jesus

by
MARGARITA HILL

Grief to Glory

Copyright © 2021 Margarita Hill

All rights reserved. No part of this publication may be reproduced, distributed, or transmitted in any form or by any means, including photocopying, recording, or other electronic or mechanical methods, without the prior written permission of the publisher, except in the case of brief quotations embodied in critical reviews and certain other noncommercial uses permitted by copyright law. For permission requests, write to the publisher, addressed "Attention: Permissions Coordinator," at the email address below.

Email requests to grieftoglory15@gmail.com.

Ordering Information: Quantity sales. Special discounts are available on quantity purchases by corporations, associations, and others. For details, contact the publisher at the email address above.

Published by Margarita Hill

Printed in the USA

First Printing, 2021

ISBN: 978-1-7366480-0-1

Dedication

For Him:

God, I thank You for helping me birth this book and my mother's legacy. Your grace is always sufficient in my life. God, I love You!

For Her:

Momma aka Peaches, I thank God that your PRESENCE speaks louder than your ABSENCE. You will always be my favorite girl. I love you Guh!!!

To Them:

Marcus, Ketomeio, Kiley, Y'all complete me in so many areas of my life and I couldn't have done any of this without y'all. I love y'all with every fiber of me.

TABLE OF CONTENTS

Introduction: Grief and Grace Have Been My Saving Grace. 7

    Prayer 14

Grief: Brief Overview 15

Stage 1: **D·E·N·I·A·L:** Aftershock... 19

    Denial Prayer 25

Stage 2: **A·N·G·E·R:** You Mad or Nah? Heck Yeah, I am Mad 27

    Anger Prayer 32

Stage 3: **B·A·R·G·A·I·N·I·N·G:** Jesus Sell Cars Now, You Get a Bargain, You Get a Bargain. Can You Just Take the Pain Away? ...33

    Bargaining Prayer 37

Stage 4: **D·E·P·R·E·S·S·I·O·N:** Retail Depression I Bought Into This While Depressed... 39

    Depression Prayer..45

Stage 5: **A·C·C·E·P·T·A·N·C·E:** I Would Like to Accept This Grief in the Name of Jesus! God Gets All the Glory.. 47

    Acceptance Prayer...50

Grief Share and Friends: Friends Experiences with Grief...............51

    From the Heart of my Good Friend Bianca Brazier 52

    Dealing with Grief in My Eyes by Jeff Cuthbertson................... 56

    From the Heart of My Sweet Sister in Christ Octavia Fomby. 58

Final Thoughts.. 61

INTRODUCTION:
Grief and Grace Have Been My Saving Grace.

Grief: "So, what the heck do I do now?"

Me: "I have no idea guh!"

Grief: "Oh, I know, you could write a book about grief."

Me: "Are you crazy I ain't no writer?"

Grief: "Guh stop playing with me, you can do this."

Me: "Says the person who I can't really stand."

Grief: "Well, ask Jesus then!"

Me: "Aye yo Jesus check it, you think I could do this."

Jesus: "Of course, you can. You can do all things through Me (Christ) who strengthens you. Right?"

Me: "Yeah, that's what the bible says so, Aight Bet!"

So, you know why we both are here right? Oh, you don't! Well, we are about to get real and raw about our grief. This book is written with authenticity and complete and utter transparency.

Are you drowning? Are you tired of being strong, or being enveloped in the darkness? Is your heart throbbing? If so, you've come to the right place. Do you know what else I am pretty sure is true? I bet I can guess that people told you to be strong, to be brave and they reminded you how strong THEY think you are/were. You don't have to tell me because I already know the answer and I am pretty sure you took that straight to the heart. You believed all the hype that you had to be strong for everyone and now you are drowning in grief without a lifeline. You let those words hit you right in the chest and now you are wearing it like a scarlet letter. Do you want to know how I know that? Well, you see it's because I allowed folks to dictate my grief. Now look at us we all over the place with no outlet because we let them same folks tell us that being STRONG trumped our grieving process. Apparently, you can't be STRONG and grieve (Tuhh I beg to differ). Oh, the lies they tell and quiet as it's kept, I am talking to both you and me. Bruh I wore that thang like a lace front with Gots2B glue.

Okay, in my Sophia's voice "PICTURE IT Hobson City, 1980 (HC4Life) Margarita A Caver was born. Listen I love me some *Golden Girls*, but on a serious note, we do have a real destination that will tell my story of how my mother transitioned to glory while I transitioned to grief. (#Glory to Grief) I am my momma's child through and through. I am the baby of 5. Yes, I am spoiled. To say that my mom and I were close would be an understatement. Our bond was unbreakable, well is unbreakable even though she lives in

Heaven and I live on earth. She's the person who I always look to for guidance. I was her shadow and happy about it. Man, my momma aka Peaches she was one of a kind and all things that made an amazing mom. She was so dedicated in her love for me, she was God's investment of love for me, she was sacrificial love, she always extended understanding, grace, and love without any conditions and ever so unapologetic and authentic in motherhood. I miss her so much, her smile, her laugh, her cooking, I even miss her cussing me out (ha, ha, ha). To know her is to love her because you couldn't help it. She had a way about her that was just as unique and special as she is/was. She gave you the right amount of love, but please don't play with her because she would give you your whole life. My momma did not play the radio. She would get you together real quick and then feed you. She raised my brother Keith and me as a single mom. My older siblings were already adults living on their own. She raised us very well even though it was not always under the best circumstances. There were hard times and heartache along the way, but she always came through for us. I thank God for who she is/was to us. She loved us like no other and she nurtured us with the right amount of cuss words and love. (Yes, my momma invented cuss words ha, ha, seriously she had the gift of cussing) I know that sounds crazy to say but it's the truth. She was by far my favorite person and we were just like peas and carrots always together. In high school, I spent more time with her and her friends than I did with my own. She was just that dope. She wasn't just our mom she was everyone's momma and the hood loved her. If yawl could have seen how many of my brother's friends ran away to our house just for a dose of her love you would be amazed. She was the best-fried chicken fryer, red velvet cake baker, chicken salad making, and the absolute best cook in the world. Oh, and she would knock you down trying to get to bingo or play cards with her friends. She made sure I knew that I was the best thing since sliced bread and the most beautiful chocolate drop in the world. So much of me wanted to be just like her as a mom. Oh, don't get it twisted I still do. She always gave God all the glory. Despite all of her health issues she constantly showed up for her kids and grandkids. There was never any lack of love, and you guessed it, she cussed us out. It was all love. If she didn't cuss you out, she didn't like you. (Don't judge my momma, judge your own momma) We had a lot of rough, but super blessed times because God always showed up for us. I remember when I got pregnant in college and I was so scared to tell her. Yawl I went to college and got the freshman 9 months instead of the freshman 15/30. When I finally got the nerve to tell her, she stopped me and said I was just waiting for you to tell me. I already knew. So, imagine the shock on my face when I asked how you know. She said because I know my child (But God) thank You, Jesus! She never made me feel bad about God's plan for me. (Won't He do it? Yes, He will if you let Him) She made it plain and clear that there will be no abortion in my future and this baby would be blessed. My God was she right. He's 21 now and in the army. My momma's grace has carried us even in her physical absence. I know she is up there getting on God's nerve about me and my kids. I know this because I know with my whole heart, she is the reason that I have my husband and daughter. She probably told God please send my baby someone to love her just as much as I do and look what God did He sent them when Ketomeio and I needed them the most. Although my husband hasn't had much experience with grief as I have, he's soothed and nurtured me through it. My momma and God be holding me down from Heaven and I am so grateful for her omnipresence from Glory (aka Heaven). When God called her to Heaven it took so much out of me. I was pissed, hurt, broken, jealous of those who still had their moms, devastated, and lonely. I remember feeling like there's no way I can survive this. How am I supposed to live in a world where my mother no longer exists in the physical? God, I'ma really need you because I'm lost. How do I go on without her? My heart felt like it was shattered into a million pieces. Like God, you really out here snatching people's mamas why? Do You not understand the magnitude of this loss for me? Like this woman is my everything, I am who I am because of who she was. Thanks a lot, Jesus! (I hope yawl know that was sarcasm.) There was nothing at that moment to be thankful for even though now I can kinda see where God was coming from, yet I still struggle with it. I mean I know that God needs us and wants us, but I needed and wanted my mother too. God, you got me out here looking crazy in these grief streets without my momma. Thank God some of my momma's prayers are coming to pass in and through this book.

OK, and before we go any further, I know you're probably wondering how I came to write this book. Well God kinda (not kinda He did) dropped it in my spirit to do this and listen I know I got on His nerves with my resistance. I would be remiss to not mention my accountability team who pushed me to get this done (I love yawl). I mean this book has been super therapeutic for me but also has been the opening of my Pandora grief box. Did I want to write this book? Nah, but I'm in a season of obedience and fully submitting to God's will. God's will has me writing this book. So, for what seems like the entire time that I have been grieving my friends think that I'm the poster child for grief. ("How Sway how?") I don't know but every time someone loses their mother people be like can you please talk to them or share some wisdom with them. (Face Palm) I'm like yo I'm still struggling with my grief and I can only share my experience. So, what do I do? I try to be a listening ear for those who ask me to or a shoulder to lean on because I know how lonely this grief space can be. I've been told a time or two that I am wise beyond my years. The old folks used to say I have an old soul. So here I am in this healing space writing this book to further my healing space and I hope and pray that you find your healing in this space. So, let's do this, let's get this healing process on.

So, here's what I need you to know about my journey with grief. Grief wrecked me, Grief consumed me, and some days it still does. However, that's okay, you know why? It's because you don't have to be the strong one and neither do I.

Prayer

Dear God,

I invite you and everyone reading into this book with the precious love of Jesus. I pray that you will find laughs, peace, love, and understanding. Aside from that I hope and pray that you find some healing and see yourself through the eyes of God who loves you and all your grief. Amen

GRIEF:
Brief Overview

So according to the world wide web (aka the innanet-internet), there are five stages of grief. It can be said that not everyone will experience all five stages nor will they go through them in a certain pattern or order. Grief is very fluid, ever-changing, heavy, nonlinear, individualized, unique, and reflective of your relationship with the person you are grieving. It is pain and love intertwined and woven together in heartache and despair. You can't put grief in a box, there is no rhyme or reason as to how it flows through you. The five stages of grief can be very inadequate in describing the roller coaster ride that is grief. Like ion even like rollercoasters yall. Who would get on something that has their bodies jerking and slamming all the while their heart is dropping into the stomach? Nah, son not me!! Let me off. OKAY, back to my point, I was in for a rude awakening thinking that grief was supposed to happen in some pattern or stages in some numerical order. It's like oh 1st you're going to be in denial about the person dying. **SIDEBAR:** (Sike, because nothing felt more real than seeing her lifeless body on that bed in the hospital)

Those thoughts and feelings were short-lived and manifested differently. During the denial stage, my denial involved my relationship with God and the spirit of why.

Then after I was supposedly out of denial, I will be angry, and my God was I angry. **SIDEBAR**: (Jesus fix it.) Oh, and then I am supposed to bargain with God to send her back to me. **SIDEBAR**: (Duh, it doesn't work like that).

Oh and now since I can't bargain with God about bringing her back, here come bargains little ugly cousin depression. I can't stand depression little snaggle tooth tale. Man, depression can kick rocks barefooted. It took so much from me and still does and that's okay. God is getting all the glory in the end. I know I've come out on the other side of depression, but it likes to show up like the auntie nobody likes because she always wanna borrow money. **SIDEBAR**: (Ain't God good, Thank You, Jesus, for Your covering.)

Now last but certainly not least is acceptance. I am now supposed to be at the place where I have fully accepted that not only you are gone but you're never coming back to Earth. I mean I am okay, but I am not okay. **SIDEBAR**: (Yawl know what I mean.)

Acceptance challenged me to create a new reality with my relationship with my mom and the relationship I have with grief.

Grief is just as much about holding on as it is letting go. Grief can be completely exhausting and a heavy burden to carry and full of high and lows. Grief can sometimes feel like an open wound that doesn't seem to quite heal and that's okay. **SIDEBAR:** (One day at a time.)

Grief can affect you mentally, physically, emotionally, financially, and spiritually. Your heart and mind can seem to be at war. Your mind knows that they are gone, and your heart is having trouble accepting that reality. For me, I've always felt like part of who I am and who I strive to be, now lives in Heaven. It's like the love of my mom and all that she is/was coupled with the pain of her death was pulling my heart into pieces. My grief has felt like a dry and empty well expecting to be filled but instead, it felt like sinking sand.

Grief began to feel like a Japanese earthquake where the aftershocks kept coming and I don't know when they will stop or how long they will last. Grief may never be a closed-door for you but something you can walk through better than you entered. It seems as if grief has become my badge of honor like I was the police. **SIDEBAR:** (Not by choice, I ain't bout that life.)

Well apparently, I am because I am writing this book and helping us heal. Ahh, I see what you did there God. My first real glimpse into grief even though this was mild compared to the loss of my mom. It was when I had to watch my father take his last breath, I realized how it worked. This act led to riding the huge never-ending rollercoaster called grief. Yawl already know how much I hate rollercoasters. Watching someone take their last breath is something that stays with you forever. At that moment you can't begin to fathom the huge impact it will have on your life. I just knew that I would be okay, and I would bounce back from this. Despite not having a great relationship with my father it still bruised me in a way I am not sure if it will ever heal. This is why I can say for me the five stages of grief are very inadequate in describing the roller coaster ride I've been riding. Grief affected my worldview on life, love, happiness, sadness, anger, and everything in between. I felt as though I had some kind of traumatic brain injury that nobody could fix. **SIDEBAR:** (I am not diminishing the capacity of someone who has a TBI) BUT GOD! My God, did I want it fixed because I was exhausted! Now let's talk about denial!

Stage 1:
D·E·N·I·A·L:
Aftershock

Me: "Am I in denial?"

Grief: "Just a little bit."

Me: "What you mean just a little bit?"

Grief: "Just what I said guh!"

Me: "Man, you play all day."

Grief: "Listen, I said a little bit because you know she is gone but you felt some kind of way towards God and how He felt about you."

Me: "You right ion understand why she didn't tell God, no and He left me with this pain."

Jesus: "Now you know darn well you can't tell our Daddy no, He doesn't play that."

Me: "Yeah, but still…"

Jesus: 'Listen our father will reveal to you His purpose in her death soon."

Me: "Look bruh I need to know now not later."

Jesus: "Patience is a virtue."

Me: "Man, I wanna hear none of that you are talking."

Grief: "You gone learn today!"

Me: "Shut up Grief!"

Jesus: "Be nice Margarita."

Me: "Man let me gone tell the people how I experienced denial."

Jesus: "You got this!"

Me: "Let's see!"

DENIAL: {a refusal to give or agree to something asked for; a refusal to admit the truth of the accusation; a refusal to accept or believe in someone or something}.

Honestly was I really in denial, I mean I heard the doctor say she was gone as I slid down the wall of the hospital at Cape Fear Valley. They even said I could see her once she was cleaned up. She still felt so much alive, her body was still warm and that smirk she wore faithfully was there on her face. I remember rubbing her hands and then her face and asking her not to leave me. **SIDEBAR:** (It was evident that she was gone). I couldn't do life without her and who was going to help me with "the boy" aka my son Ketomeio. Man listen this lady was my everything in human form, all that I am and strive to be was because of her. **SIDEBAR:** (I know I already said that, but I need yawl to feel the magnitude of her in my eyes).

So maybe she's not gone, I will wake up and she will be here. I mean God did You just take my Momma? I know that we all have our day and time, but You couldn't wait? Nah, this ain't where it's at Jesus. I need my momma Yo! I thought we were better than this Lord, but I guess not. You play way too much, and I don't think this is funny so gone and send her, her cigarettes, and cigarette pouch back down here. Plus, God you know my momma don't play about these grandbabies and she wouldn't dare let you take her from them. **SIDEBAR:** (I know you can't let God do anything.)

We all about to be lost. Bruh, so my momma was just gone, just like that. We are two peas in a pod when you see one you see the other. How will I function without her? What are we going to do without her? As we rode back to my brother Keith and his then-wife Shanda's house the song ribbon in the sky by Stevie Wonder played and it hit me in the chest like a ton of bricks. I knew that was God's confirmation that she is really gone. She loved that song. As all three of us laid in one bed trying to figure out how we were going to tell our kids that their granny was gone had me buggin'. I was like Jesus this is so wrong on so many levels, these kids love they granny and now we have to break their hearts. Look Jesus I need you to explain to me how breaking these kids' hearts will serve a purpose in my momma's death. It was like I was having an out-of-body experience and watch my life roll on by. My feelings toward her death left me in denial about how Jesus felt about me. You can't possibly love me and died for me but took my momma. Oh, I feel the judgment in my spirit and you telling me don't question God, but how am I supposed to get answers if I don't ask questions. Yeah, I see your face. **SIDEBAR:** (Irrational thinking at its finest, I know.)

Even as I traveled to Alabama and throughout the funeral and on to the cemetery none of it seem real. It was all a blur, and I don't remember much about that day. I just knew that I was on an episode of PUNK'D and Ashton Kutcher was going to jump out. But he never came. Jesus be fence because once I made it back to North Carolina denial was no longer a thing, but reality quickly set in. So, Lord, you just gone let me leave my momma out there at the cemetery by herself. I know she cold and lonely. I need to go get her. **SIDEBAR:** (I knew that it was only her physical body there because her spirit was in heaven), but that's how I felt at the time, you feel me on that right? I was really upset though because she ain't got no cigarettes or Coca-Cola, she was gone be mad. God, my life is never going to be the same, is it? The breakdown that came from this revelation nearly broke me. **SIDEBAR:** (Okay it did break me for a long time.)

Yet I hid it from everyone because everyone was telling me how **STRONG** I was, and they were seriously wrong. Like seriously wanted to scream at the top of my lungs I am not **STRONG.** This is where I allowed the word STRONG to infiltrate my entire experience with grief moving forward. People would say "Oh you're so strong, after all, you've been through you are still pushing through life. You look so good and healthy." I wanted to scream because on the inside I was drowning in my thoughts, regrets, shoulda, coulda, and woulda. Yet no one wanted to hear that. It's like no one wants to hear your ugly side of grief because they don't know how to handle it.

The truth of the matter was I was drowning in the ocean and the waves and tide were taking me further and further away from the shore. It felt like seaweed was wrapped around my feet holding me hostage. But folks didn't wanna hear that from me. They just wanna hear that I am fine, so they can say oh I am praying you. **SIDEBAR**: (That was the prayer.)

You know why, because grief is messy, and it makes people so uncomfortable to talk about. I allowed the word strong to stifle my grief and keep me in a state of denial that I was fine. Listen I was not fine because I couldn't grieve the way I needed because I had to be STRONG for my son, my family, and friends, but guess what I didn't have to, but I let others dictate my process when I shouldn't have. **SIDEBAR:** (That won't happen again!)

You can't heal from what you don't acknowledge. I was in denial about how much fear her death had taken up residence in my heart, mind, and soul. God, what if I die and leave my son here to pick up the pieces like I am trying to do. I mean shoot let's be honest I'm grown and I'm on the struggle bus and still need my mom even at the ripe age of 26. Would he fear death like me because I can't fathom how she could leave me like this? **SIDEBAR:** (I know I shouldn't fear death because it's all a part of God's plan...it was the grief talking)

Denial of any form can be such a surreal space and place to be in. It comes and goes with lots of crazy thoughts and emotions. It can have your emotions all over the place and you do your best to hide it. **SIDEBAR:** (But you can't hide from God, he sees it.)

You try to hide the hurt and pain by not acknowledging how strong it is. It's like you're in denial about what this loss has done to you mentally, physically, emotionally, and spiritually, but don't be in so much denial that you resist God's outstretched hand leading you to the truth and giving you peace. Now just as peace in this area rolled in that heifer anger pulled up on me. Here we go and guess what I was mad as hell I was so angry. So, let's talk about it, but first, let's pray about denial.

DENIAL PRAYER

God, we come to You humbly as we know how. My God, please help save us from this sinking sand. God our spirits are crushed by grief and our hearts are broken by this loss. Heal us Oh Lord, we need You now more than ever. We just can't wrap our minds around this loss and what purpose it serves because we need them, Lord. We can't live this life without them, Lord. Lord, please come save us from this brokenness. God, it's so hard to remember Your love for us when we feel this loneliness please encourage our heart and mind. God, it's so painful right now to sit with this truth and pain. God, we don't want to live in this everlasting cycle of pain and grief. God, we've been here so long please release us from this stronghold. God, we are crying out to you. Please hear our cry and wipe our tears. In your word, it says that You are our protection and our strength. You will always help in the time of trouble. Lord, please help us and be our protection and strength in your son Jesus name. (Psalms 46:1) Amen!

STAGE 2:
A·N·G·E·R:
You Mad or Nah? Heck Yeah, I am Mad

Grief: "You mad or nah?"

Me: "You know you make me sick right?"

Grief: "Yeah, Yeah..."

Me: "Ugh!"

Jesus: "What's going on here?"

Me: "Grief being her usual worrisome self and making me mad."

Grief: "What I do?"

Me: "Like you don't know."

Jesus: "Why you so angry?"

Me: "Yawl really gone act like God didn't just take my momma?"

Jesus: "Oh..."

Me: "Yeah, that's what I thought."

Jesus: "You know how God works and..."

Me: "You betta not finish that sentence."

Grief: "So, you just gone let her say that to you, Jesus?"

Jesus: "Yeah, I can understand her anger and I'm gone let her be great right now."

Me: "Thanks, I guess... Well, I guess I will tell you exactly why I'm angry so here we go.

What I don't understand is why you didn't cuss God out like you did us? **SIDEBAR:** (Aye what I tell yall about that judging me and my momma, judge your momma we good over here.) She probably did and He put her in time out. Real talk, I know she was like God listen you have to send me back down there. Margarita and Keith need me to help them with dem kids. My momma was the original savage. **SIDEBAR:** (I know why she didn't because you ain't supposed to cuss God duh!)

So, when anger pulled up on me my question to my Momma was why didn't you tell Him you didn't want to go? **SIDEBAR:** (Duh! It doesn't work like that.) I was so mad at everyone. Yep, I was mad at God, my siblings, the kids, my friends. **SIDEBAR:** (Yeah her, her, him, them, everybody...in my Kelly Rowland voice.)

Yo, and please don't tell me I shouldn't be angry because she in a better place. I found no comfort in that. Man, do you know how stupid that sounds to someone who's missing their loved one who just died? (Yeah, that part) Man, shut up! **SIDEBAR:** (Ain't no better place than being with us.)

That was my flesh and the anger talking because I know being with Jesus trumps everything else. I was pissed, she left me here and didn't even say goodbye or anything just gone. My anger was like an anchor holding a boat in place, so it doesn't drift out into the water. My anger made me reckless with my life due to the people, places, and things that I allowed to enter my sacred place. **SIDEBAR:** (My entire being but especially my heart.)

I was out there putting on a show pretending I wasn't angry. Why? Apparently, you can't be angry and STRONG. **SIDEBAR:** (Go figure.) Now truth be told I didn't want to be neither I didn't want to be angry, and I didn't want to be strong, but yawl already know what I wanted. Yes, I wanted my momma. The spirit of anger had me so out of pocket that I was even reckless with my motherhood. Bruh I was out here wilding out and living "quote-unquote"my best life. **SIDEBAR:** (Lies all Lies!)

I was in fact not living my best life because I was so angry with God, I couldn't see my behavior for what it was. Like if God really loved me then why am I in so much pain and so angry. I allowed my anger to make me feel like I deserve the craziness that I was bringing into my world. I remember being so angry with siblings that I wouldn't talk to them for weeks at a time. In my mind, they had more time with her and got to be with her longer. She was able to witness them get married and have children. I didn't get to experience her seeing me get married and have another child. Plus, they don't seem as sad and heartbroken as I was, they don't miss her as I do. **SIDEBAR:** (Not true at all, everyone's grief looks different.)

I mean the audacity of God to take her from me at 25 when He knew that I needed her, but he ain't even care. **SIDEBAR:** (Of course, He did.) I was so angry I believed He stopped caring about me because why else would He do it. Being knee-deep in your grief can take your mind places you never wanna visit again. Oh, But GOD, God's love doesn't operate in restraints. It was my anger and bad attitude that kept me in bondage and in this angry space that I refuse to let go, but God saw fit for me to come out on the other side. Anger makes you feel like you have something to hold on to because the numbness of grief can take your breath away and make it hard to breathe. I found it so hard to be happy about anything when I was no longer able to share the same space with my momma.

Anger is so much easier than happiness when you're grieving. It was like I was in this grief hangover and I couldn't see through the fogginess of anger. Don't fear the rage and sadness it all serves a purpose. Try not to rush the process. **SIDEBAR:** (Yeah right, I want off this rollercoaster.)

Yeah, I know you do too, and just as I thought I was about to get off the ride the conductor said next step bargain town. I mean what the heck is bargain town. I mean do they got a sale on tickets to heaven so you can see your loved one. For real doe that's the only reason why I want to go to bargain town, but guess what bargain town does not sell tickets to heaven. So, what I found out is that in bargain town we are out here treating God like a car salesman. (Help us, Lord!)

Anger Prayer

God. open up our hearts and usher out this unhinged feeling of anger. Anger has no place in our hearts and minds, yet we feel completely submerged into it. God, we call for a release that only You can grant. God, release us from this fear of abandonment and the fire that resides in our bellies. God, release us from these destructive thoughts that plague our entire being. God, please help us come to a peaceful and healthy understanding of this anger. Lord God, we want You to be the anchor for our souls, not this anger that has taken root in us. God, it says in Your word that You keep track of our sorrows and You value our tears. God help us to see You through the tears and know that we are not alone in our anger and grief. God, we are standing on Your word. Your word says for Your anger is but for a moment, and Your favor is for a lifetime. Weeping may endure for the night, but joy comes with the morning. God heal our anger like only You can and give us joy. In Your Son Jesus name. Amen!

STAGE 3:
B·A·R·G·A·I·N·I·N·G:
Jesus Sell Cars Now, You Get a Bargain, You Get a Bargain. Can You Just Take the Pain Away?

Me: "So, people really be thinking God a car salesman?"

Grief: "What you mean?"

Me: "They be bargaining with God about their loved ones."

Grief: "Girl yes!"

Me: "Wow!"

Grief: "What you saying wow for, you didn't bargain in the traditional sense but you did try to promise something for something."

Me: "Guh hush, you think you know everything."

Jesus: "Margarita you know she right?"

Me: "Yes, but she always in my business."

Jesus: "Y'all getting on my nerves."

Me: "My bad Jesus, I am sorry, she just irks my soul."

Grief: "Same, same."

Me: "Whatever!"

Jesus: "You know our Father doesn't operate in the let's make a deal scheme of things."

Me: "Yeah, I know but I tried it anyway."

Grief: "Yep, you tried it."

Me: "Guh... (shaking my head) anyway let's talk about bargaining with God and how it doesn't work."

Bargaining with God is that a thing? I mean I've never known God to play let's make a deal. You either step into his will or you don't. Bargaining can take on many forms. During this time in my grief, I tried not to play the what-if game. What if this or what if that even though we all know that when it's your time, it's your time. For me, I tried to promise God that if he healed me from this hurt and pain that I would fully submit to His will for my life. **SIDEBAR:** (Whew Chile, God was like you should want to submit to me with or without this grief but GO AWF GUH.)

Grief can make you physically ill, mentally unstable, emotionally damaged, and spiritually spent. Bargaining makes you feel like you have control over the situation when in actuality you don't. It makes you feel like you should have done things differently or things would be different if this happened. Your mind is wrestling with the truth and control. There is no right or wrong way to grieve. Thinking that you can bargain with

God can lead you into deep despair set on an unhealthy terrain. I found myself unbalanced and unstable during this time. There's a lot of regret in this season, in which you try to find balance while offering something up to God. **SIDEBAR:** (Jesus was sick of me, I know I got on his nerves.)

I was apprehended into the spirit of why. Like seriously why would you do this to me and shatter me? Why wouldn't You save her? Why didn't You allow me to say goodbye? Why would You allow me to be in this pain? Why can't this be over already? Bargaining had me raw and bitter making me think that my faith and grief were enemies. Matthew 5:4 says, "They are blessed who grieve for God will comfort them." I wanted to stop negotiating with God and anchor myself in His peace, love, and light. Remember that it's okay to live authentically in your grief and allow people to see the real and uncomfortable side of grief. God wants us to heal and not feel like the only way we get what want is to bargain and negotiate with Him. **SIDEBAR:** (Honey, He ain't no car salesman.)

See what I mean about bargain town. He knows exactly what my heart, mind, and soul desires from Him. God was on me hard during this season. He was like listen stop trying to bargain with Me because what's done is done. He said let me help you heal and become whole again and I was like but, but......WHY? It was then I realize that tossing, turning, and wrestling with WHY caused me to find more fault not only in myself but also in God. **SIDEBAR:** (I know I was wrong, and God has no faults.)

God didn't need me to offer Him anything, He has everything He needs and if He wanted something to change, He would change it. You can't gain control over something you never had control over anyway. Bargaining with God will not render you successful. Don't be so desperate for control that you lose all sense of the reality that God always has the final say. Oh boy here comes depression let me go hide.... Oh no it found me. (come out, come out wherever you are) Dang, it.

Bargaining Prayer

Father God, we are in desperate need of Your strength right now. We are not sure how to move forward in this grief space. Lord, we are clinging to all things that remind us of our loved ones. God, we are running to You with tear-stained faces, heavy hearts, mind racing, and our souls are full of despair. God, take this from us we don't want. How could You think we want this? God how do we find this strength that Your word speaks of. God, please give it to us, we need it like running water. God, we are running to You with open arms we need You to catch us. God, show us this loving faith and give us Your mercy for we are hurting Lord. We need You right now, all of You God. Rescue us from this pain, hurt, and despair. We are calling out to You please hear our cries Lord. Father can You hear us, can you feel us we are crying out for You in anguish. God, help our hearts and mind. We are wrestling with how You could let this happen and if we could have done something to change the outcome. God, couldn't You have taken someone else. We need You to wrap Your arms around us and comfort us, Lord God. We pray these things over us in Your Son's Jesus name!

Amen!

STAGE 4:
D·E·P·R·E·S·S·I·O·N:
Retail Depression I Bought Into This While Depressed.

Grief: "How you feeling?"

Me: "You already know I am depressed about my momma."

Grief: "Yeah, I figured you still were."

Me: "So why did you even ask? I swear you work my nerves guh."

Grief: "Look, I just wanted to see if anything had changed?"

Me: "You know it hasn't, you trying to be funny."

Grief: "Nah, I'm not."

Jesus: "What yawl fussing about now?"

Me: "Grief always saying stuff and asking stupid questions."

Jesus: "Well maybe she is concerned about you."

Me: "Concerned about me, she partly the cause of me being depressed."

Jesus: "Yeah, but this is all a part of the process."

Me: "Well, I ain't ask for this process no way so just let me be depressed."

Jesus: "You think I am about to let you buy into this whole, you will be depressed your whole life because your Momma died?"

Me: "Why not? It's not like I will be happy again without her."

Jesus: "You do know who our Father is right?"

Me: "Yes, I do but..."

Jesus: "First of all, ain't no BUT with our Father...so just watch Him bring you out on the other side."

Me: "Alright I trust yawl (okay sometimes) I am working on it."

Jesus: "We about to refund your depression back to where it came from."

Me: "Let's do this!"

Depression gets a bad reputation like a stripper on the pole. **SIDEBAR:** (I know what you are thinking stripper, pole, Jesus, and depression don't go together. As I said before don't judge me, judge yourself.)

Oh, but it does, and it got your attention. Now Depression is a DISEASE like it's DIS-EASE because your spirit isn't at ease. It's because your spirit is fighting a life and death situation. It is like a flesh-eating disease and it's literally eating you alive. Depression is the art of disguise. It has you disguising your darkness under the façade of I'm okay, I'm fine, and I'm happy! Depression coupled with grief doesn't seem to fit people's narrative on if it's a disease or not. I had to learn to stop letting people tell me about my grief and depression. Y'all would be looking at people sideways if they told someone who has asthma, "Do not use your inhaler" or someone who has high blood pressure, "Do not take your medicine." So, don't you dare tell me how to manage my grief or how I should be over someone's death by now. By whose standards does grief have a timeline on how long it lasts. Depression is more severe than just being sad, unmotivated, and the feeling of loneliness. Depression can make you feel like you're in a constant state of chaos. It makes the simplest task so overwhelming. For me, depression started when I realize that my ultimate support system was gone and feeling completely overwhelmed along with the anxiety of it all. I couldn't do anything but cry and hyperventilate. Yawl I didn't even have any energy to simply be anything. I couldn't be happy, be sad, or be content because all I wanted to be was left alone.

Yet, I couldn't do any of that because I had responsibilities despite being swallowed up by the darkness of my grief and depression. Listen, yawl the spirit of depression is real out here in these grief streets. Depression had me going from one moment of feeling nothing to feeling every emotion all at once and bawling my eyes out. God, please make it stop!! I remember not being able to see mothers-daughters out and about without feeling anger and sadness. Don't get me wrong it was beautiful to see but a painful and heartbreaking reminder of my loss.

Most people think that depression looks like oh I am sad and so I am going to go listen to sad music, or it's let me go eat my feelings or walk in the rain and cry. Bruh depression didn't and still doesn't look like that for me. Although I am sure that it looks like that for a lot of people. All I could do is say to God, "please help me to get back to me." Lord, I don't even know who I am right now. I can't see beyond the fog, it's so hard to see through my depression. I don't want this life God please take this from me. Not only was depression running rampant in my spirit, but her sister, anxiety kept rearing her ugly bald-head tail in my spirit and boffum started to wreak havoc on my life. The depressive state of knowing that she was gone, and I was left all alone amped up my anxiety. It felt as though the anxiety of depression renders me unable to function. My depression and anxiety came out as so much more than sadness and anxiousness. It showed up in the form of migraines, insomnia, carelessness, starvation, body aches, worry, fear, and uneasiness. I was physically and emotionally numb to life but in a functioning state. I only wanted to do the things I had to do because I had to take care of myself and my child. Depression tried to take my life and anxiety tried to drown me. Depression made me feel alone in my grief. **SIDEBAR:** (I know that God is always there, and He cares about me and loves me.)

God loves me like no one else does. My depression and anxiety wouldn't even let me find peace and comfort in His words. I was seriously high key walking around depressed and anxious and I know that was displeasing to God. The depression and emptiness of grief had me climbing the walls and ready to leave it all beyond. I mean ion wanna go on without my Momma, my life will never be the same and I am not okay with that. This season in my grief altered my life and changed my entire outlook on life, love, and God. There's a space that can't be filled until I get to heaven and see my mom again. I realize that my healing is a process, and it could have happened instantaneously, or it could take years. **SIDEBAR:** (As you can see it's been 15 years and I am still healing so that's God's will for my grief.)

God has chosen this very path for me even though it's painful, heart-wrenching, emotionally, spiritually, physically, and mentally draining He's with me and I find comfort in that. It hasn't been easy living amid grief, depression, and anxiety knowing Satan is using it as a weapon to keep me bound. Man, Satan ol' raggedy bald-headed-self make me sick. Even though he thought he had me God reminded me that even on my rough days I have to remember that God's presence in my life is His promise to me. **SIDEBAR:** (Even when I was mad at him (God).)

Aye, I can't believe I am about to say this, but everything wasn't the devil some of it was God growing me in my walk with Him. **SIDEBAR:** (Ion care if the devil baldheaded self knows that I said this I ain't scared of him.)

I've learned that it's okay to have moments in your grief but don't stay there and most definitely don't unpack there because it will be hard to leave. I remember being with people yet feeling alone because people didn't understand my need to have my moments. They didn't want to hear that I was hurting, in pain and my heart was so heavy. I remember thinking UGH I HATE IT HERE! Like for real God this how You do me, your favorite child. Man, this ain't it and I don't remember signing up for any of this. You ain't even have to put me through all this, BUT God allowed me to find strength in my depression and sparks of joy. I had to dig deep inside of myself and pull myself out to not end up in the sunken place aka depression city. Lord, I don't know if I would ever accept this but help me create a new reality where You get all the glory. Now let's talk about accepting that they're gone.

DEPRESSION PRAYER

God by faith we are petitioning that we no longer want to live this life full of depression and tribulations. God this hardship and suffering have become too much. God, we wanna let depression go but we don't know how. We've been reading our bible and studying Your word but finding no comfort. Lord, we are seeking Your comfort. God Your word says that You will renew my strength and mount me with wings, and we shall run and not be weary. God help us to not be weary. Lord God, it says in Your Word that we can Come to You, all who labor and are heavy laden, and you will give us rest. God, we are so tired, and we desire to be able to rest in You and lay our heads on Your lap so we can feel at peace. God do you know how heavy this burden has been to bear. We are seeking You above all else. We surrender our grief to You oh God. We claim healing for our souls in Your Son's Jesus name. Amen!!

STAGE 5:
A·C·C·E·P·T·A·N·C·E:
I Would Like to Accept This Grief in the Name of Jesus! God Gets All the Glory

Grief: "You know with time you are gone be alright right?"

Me: "What is you talking about Guh?"

Grief: "You know as time goes on you will be just fine without your mother."

Me: "Have you lost your mind chile? I will not be okay with this."

Grief: "You have to accept the fact that she's gone."

Me: "I ain't gotta do nothing but stay black and die."

Grief: "Man...Jesus come get this girl."

Me: "Don't be calling Jesus on me, I am mad at Him too!"

Jesus: "Listen I thought we were on better terms by now?"

Me: "Nah, You know how grief does, it comes and goes."

Jesus: "Yes, I'm fully aware of how you and grief get down."

Me: "What's that supposed to mean?"

Jesus: "It just means yawl aren't on the best of terms."

Me: "Oh, okay I was about to say I know You not on her side."

Jesus: "Nope I am on our father's side."

Me: "As we all should be, it's just I am trying to find a way to accept this and makes things a little more bearable."

Jesus: "No worries, me and our father have you covered even when don't think we do."

Me: "Well, show me what yawl got because I am struggling to accept this."

Jesus: "We got you as always."

You know how the saying goes "time heals all wounds" it doesn't. It's a complete lie that people tell you when they try to get you to accept something that hurts. Time doesn't always heal it just becomes an acceptance and we have to live with it. I mean we all understand that this person is gone, and you try to continue to get things back to normal the best you can. Honestly, how do you come to grips with accepting their death? Have I come to grips with accepting her death? I would love to say yes but that would be a lie. Even though it's been 15 years it still feels like yesterday. Acceptance can make you think you're OK with their death but in actuality, it's about creating a new reality. As you all know reality sometimes is hard to accept no matter how much is staring you in the face.

I had to learn to embrace the present and look forward to the future even though my heart was aching. Life has forever changed for me so I'm trying to find the love that I feel like I lost with the death of my mother in this new reality. Kubler-Ross says "acceptance is often confused with the notion of it being alright or ok with what happened to your loved one." Now yawl knows darn well most of us will not ever be ok or all good about the loss of our loved ones.

Acceptance for me felt like I had to rebrand myself and my relationship with my mother. Since she was no longer here, I had to figure out a way to fill her presence without being able to physically see her. So, what does that look like for me well she loved to cook and so I fell in love with cooking. She loved her grandbabies, so, I've built an unbreakable bond with my nieces and nephews. I celebrate her every month by doing something that she loved to do. I sleep in her nightgowns; I call her friends and reminisce on who she was to us. I silence the noise so I can hear her voice and I ask God to allow her to meet me in my dreams and just hold me. Although I haven't fully embraced the acceptance part of this journey, I have found that in some instances when I do it's a gift from God. This has been super hard because this experience has been brutal and painful. Yet God has given me great wisdom even during my grief. Ion know who they are but THEY say that acceptance is your full-circle moment. I don't know that to be true but what I do know is that for me to grow into the woman she raised me to be she had to go. I find myself constantly praying the serenity prayer in this season.

Acceptance Prayer

God, grant me the serenity to accept the things I cannot change, the courage to change the things I can, and the wisdom to know the difference. Living one day at a time, enjoying one moment at a time; accepting hardship as a pathway to peace; Taking, as Jesus did, this sinful world as it is, not as I would have it; trusting that You will make all things right if I surrender to Your will; so that I may be reasonably happy in this life and supremely happy with You forever in the next. Amen.

GRIEF SHARE AND FRIENDS: FRIENDS EXPERIENCES WITH GRIEF

Thank you all for being brave enough to share your grieving heart with me and all who read this book. You are a true blessing from God. I know that there will be a lot of people healed from your words. I love you, my friends.

From the Heart of my Good Friend Bianca Brazier

The definition of grief is, "A deep sorrow, especially that is caused by someone's death." I learned in the School of Social work that there are 5 stages of grief. 1. Denial 2. Anger. 3. Bargaining. 4. Depression 5. Acceptance.

I lost my mother in March 2004, but I began grieving before she left this earth. In September of 2001, my mother was diagnosed with Lung Cancer. I was unaware at the time, but she was given a prognosis of 6 months to live. Amazingly, we were given more time with her.

She began Chemotherapy soon after her diagnosis. It was a long and difficult process, but she seemed fine to me on the outside. I was 19 so I was just living life and not processing what she was going through. I was doing things she was not happy about or proud of and we clashed a great deal. In 2003, months after finding out, I informed her I was pregnant. She was very disappointed in me because she wanted more for me than to be an unwed mother at a young age. She wanted me to graduate from college, get married, and start a family. She eventually came to terms with it and when my daughter was born, she was over the moon for her.

My mother's cancer was in remission and things were fine. She had even attended her first Relay for Life event as a survivor. That would not last long though. December of 2003, she came to me and told me that the cancer was back and because it had spread to her liver there was nothing the doctors could do. She was honest and upfront with me this time and told me she did not know how long it would be, but that it would not be long. This was devastating to me. I believe this is when I experienced the first stage of grief, denial. Surely there was something that could be done. She discussed the possibility of participating in an experimental treatment at Vanderbilt, but never went through with it. I was angry about it because how could you not try. Again, selfish 21-year-old me only thinking about how much I need her, not about the fact she was tired and possibly ready.

I watched her health deteriorate as the months went on. I grieved for the loss of her as the person she once was. I cried for her daily as if she were already gone. I could not keep food down and my stomach was upset all of the time. I was losing weight and was not healthy at all due to the stress. Even as her health was failing her, and her life was slipping away, she was still concerned about me. She would tell me I had to stop making myself sick, I had to be healthy for Tristan, and that she would be okay. Easier said than done. I was already picturing my life without her rather than enjoying her while she was still with me. This is what anger and depression look like. I had already tried bargaining and felt like God was not hearing me or answering my prayers.

As the time came closer, she had family coming to see her all of the time. One of her closest friends came from Virginia to be with her and her father came from Maryland to be with her, I think that is when it really hit me. I never wanted to be at home because seeing all of those people there with her made it seem so real and I was not ready to let go, but she was now in a wheelchair and I believe she lost her sight, so the hospice nurses said the time was coming, maybe in the next few days. She suffered a fall which was believed to have impeded the process of her organs shutting down.

March 17, 2004, which started as a normal day, turned out to be the worst day of my life. As I was on my way home, my cousin who was driving me was told to get me home as soon as possible and that is when I knew. My mother died that evening surrounded by the people who loved her the most. I was hurt because I was not there. I was hurt because I did not kiss her goodbye when I left the house that morning and that was the last time, I saw her alive.

Although the stages of grief are said to occur after your loved one is gone, I truly believe that we can begin the process when they are here. This is true for those of us who have had the misfortune of watching the ones we love to die. Some feel it is better to know and think you are prepared when you know, but I think it hurts worse. It is also my opinion that the steps of grief do not always take place in any particular order or timeframe. Grief will make you think you are just fine, but then out of now where you are bawling or just feeling down and depressed thinking about the loved one you lost.

There is no right or wrong way to deal with grief. There is no deadline of when you are to be finished grieving. I think it is a lifelong process that we just learn to deal with. We tuck it away when we need to, and we allow it to come out when it needs to. My advice would be to take it as it comes and deal with it accordingly whether that means medication, talking to a therapist or close friend, or other healthy coping mechanisms. Allow it to happen when it needs to.

Dealing with Grief in My Eyes by Jeff Cuthbertson

My grief process started in 2019 where God took me out of a 13-year career of being a probation officer. I remember coming home confuse and uncertain about my future and what to do with it. It was only God that showed me that He is calling me to the Mental Health world and where I will find personal peace in being an in-home counselor as well as a substance abuse counselor. I remember God moving in a mighty way toward the end of 2019 by increasing my clients, giving me the idea to create GOD + Therapy, and even creating speaking engagements. I was ready for 2020, the next level where big things were going to happen.

Then came the real 2020, we all know the real 2020. Covid-19 took over and provided loss in many different forms for many different people. Well for me the real 2020 took not only my mother but my grandmother as well. This was one of the biggest sneak attacks in my life. The passing of my mother brought pain that I have never experience. The 11 days of watching my mother in the ICU were extremely painful. However, just like walking into 2020, my expectations were high. My faith guided me to believe that my mother was going to walk out of the hospital completely heal and it would be a testament to the power of God. That did not happen but it did not stop God from showing His power, love, and grace.

During my grieving, God took me to a passage in the bible. God took me to Mark 4:35-40, where Jesus was in the back of the boat that was crossing to the other side of the lake, and when the disciples engaged Him after being afraid of the storm, He quieted the winds and the storm. After performing this miracle, He asked "why are you afraid? Do you not have faith in me?" In this passage, God reminded me that He is still in control. God also showed me that the promise is still the promise. Now I can live this uncertain season walking by faith not by sight by allowing my emotions to be control by the word of God and by practicing healthy self-care techniques such as journaling and practicing self-affirmations. I want to encourage you right now by saying that when dealing with grief remember to engage God in your process. Remember to always embrace those feelings never fight them. GOD BLESS!

From the Heart of My Sweet Sister in Christ Octavia Fomby.

The loss of a parent is something that I never thought in a million years that I would experience. So, you can just imagine the shock and trauma of having to bury both of my parents. My mother and father were my everything I'm the baby of 11 children, my mother's only child because by the time I came along nobody was in the house but me. From birth until August 1998 when I left for college it had only been me, Mama, and Daddy. That's all I knew we were the three amigos, they were my best friends.

My mother was the cream of the crop. When it comes to mothers it just didn't get any better. (I am biased of course) This lady was everything to me she personified beauty and grace. Her beauty (my God) I'm telling you she was the epitome of a virtuous woman. I mean the woman had it all: beauty, style, always dressed to the 9s, brains, and she was an Educator for 30 plus years. She had a sense humor, the best to ever do it. She could also sing and play the piano. You name it she could do it. Now because daddy was the sole provider it was mostly me and my momma every day all we did was talk and laugh and talk and laugh. To watch someone so full of life slowly lose who they are because of dementia and strokes is just something you can't prepare for. I mean I was her only child, and she couldn't even remember my birthday. How was I supposed to deal with that? Life as I knew it would be no more. My mother was fading away and I didn't know how to get her back. Now daddy oh he was the best daddy that a girl could ever dream of. He was a Deacon in the Lord's church, a hard worker, a humble servant, a comedian in his own right the most dressed cat this side of heaven. He had a bad pimp walk so fierce that even Jerome (AKA from *Martin*) had to take a back seat. (LMBO) For me, he was my first love all you daddy's girls know exactly what I mean. He never disrespected me, never made me feel like I was less than who God purposed me to be. He was always the perfect gentleman (well to me and my momma) and always, always, always purposefully took time to spend quality time with me. It was always just the two of us until his dying day. When it comes to daddies' Baby, he was it.

The day my mother left me September 21st, 2012 I didn't know what to think of it. Of course, the first feeling was an overwhelming sense of sadness and that was followed by anger. I felt like life was unfair because everyone else gets to have their mother. Like I know people in their 70s who are still blessed with their mothers. Here, I am at the age of 32 going to view mine in a casket. (UGH) OK so then daddy dies without running it past me first on September 9th, 2019. So now along with the aforementioned emotions comes loneliness. At least when Mama died, I still had my daddy. Now I have nobody. I am an orphan. Yes, I have a wonderful husband and three beautiful children who love me more than anything, but a parent's love can never be replaced, and neither can their presence. There are days when I feel so lonely that I don't even want to talk to anyone. Then there are days everyone around me has the joy and excitement of being with all of their family. Yet here I am having to muster up a smile and laugh so as not to be judged or put a damper on everyone else's mood. What am I supposed to do? How am I supposed to feel when normally I would call one of my parents when my days were rough. Now what do I do, who do I call now? Everyone around me still has at least one parent but me not so much as one. I feel like nobody understands. Ugh. Then I am reminded of the words of the Apostle Paul, here's what he said "for our high priest is able to understand our weakness, He was tempted in every way that we are, but he did not sin. Let us, then, feel very sure that we can come before God's throne where there is grace. There we can receive mercy and grace to help us when we need it." (Hebrews 4:15-16) This simply says to me that there is absolutely no emotion I have felt, presently feel, or will feel that Jesus, the High Priest has not felt. He knows exactly what you and I are dealing with, every pain, every fear, every tear you name it He feels it. You may say, Octavia, (that's me) what about the days when the grief overtakes me and there are no words just simply tears? He knows and understands that too. Your silence? He even hears that. So, my advice to you dear readers is to lean on the one who not only knows your pain but can do something about it. All you have is God and time! Much Love from Octavia Fomby

FINAL THOUGHTS

I've tried to force myself to get over it but boy is that hard to do when you have so many unanswered questions. I know I won't get those questions answered until I get to heaven, and then God is gone be like guh just enjoy heaven with your momma and leave me alone. **SIDEBAR:**(God funny like that.) Well, at least he is to me.

I also realized how ill-prepared I was for this journey and astronomical loss. As soon as you start to feel better and hope the happiness settles in your spirit it doesn't. It can be the simplest things that trigger you back into the spin cycle of grief. Sometimes you have to laugh to keep from crying because your life is now similar to BC/AC (before Christ and after Christ) now it's BM/AM (before momma and after momma). Geesh that's so hard to do. There are days my entire being feels heavy like I'm in a weighted blanket. Before I go, I wanted to say that for me to do this and to share this I had to tap into a place of strength to birth this book. When I tell you the birth pains that have come from pouring my heart out has been astronomical but so divinely guided. The spirit of doubt, insecurities, fear, and revisiting a place I've long to have forgotten, my God I thank You.

The loneliness that took over my spirit and soul was like a dull knife, but then I realize that my mother didn't leave me here by myself like I thought she did. Along the way, God placed so many wonderful people in my life. When I was living in North Carolina and my mother passed away I had a circle of friends who took care of me and my kid and in some ways restored my faith. I remember meeting one of my best friends Ali when our sons played on the same basketball team. I remember telling her that I had just lost my mom and I had no idea how I was going to go to school full-time, work, and take care of my child without my mom. As a single mom, I couldn't afford daycare and could barely afford a babysitter. That day I had no idea that God was planting a seed of a friendship between me and Ali. After telling her all of that she said oh girl I'll watch him after school for you, and I was like you're gonna watch my son for me and she was like yeah. She said the boys get along just fine and Ketomeio was no trouble. I said ok well I don't know how I can pay you because you know I just got this apartment. I'm working two jobs and going to school. She said oh you don't have to pay me all you have to do is buy some snacks for the boys. I was like girl you ain't said nothing but a word. How many snacks you want me to buy and she said whatever you think the boys will like. When I tell you at that moment, I was like God I'm not alone, not like I thought I was.

God reminded me that day that He would never leave me alone even when I'm angry with Him even when I don't understand Him, He always provides. There's no way I would have survived those first couple of months without my mother if it weren't for my circle of friends. My best friends Renee and Sparkal stepped in and babysat, cooked for us, got us out of the house, loved on us, and took care of us.

There was a time that I felt like grief was gonna destroy me and instead it transformed me. This journey has taught me that this is where God needs me to be right now and it's not going to always feel good. Sometimes God needs me to be uncomfortable because some of the best blessings come from uncomfortable situations. I had to learn to allow God to have his way and accept everything with my life even in this space with my grief. I also realize that it did me no good to try to hide the sadness behind my eyes or the shell of a person that I was. There was no joy, no hope, no love, no light but only darkness. God wanted so much more for me and I know my mother does too.

I'm grateful to have found strength in my grief and find ways to spark joy again. If I wanted to regain control of my grief, I had to realize that I was in charge of my narrative, not other people. I was out here letting people treat my grief like an episode of *Reading Rainbow* and tell me how the story goes. Remember to let God set the pace for this journey and slow down enough to make sure that you're hearing from Him. As long as I stay in communication with God, He will equip me to handle what's ahead.

Even though I'm nowhere near where I would like to be in my grief journey. God is teaching me how to live above my circumstances even when life is full of clutter, debris, depression, anxiety, and grief. The Bible says "God stays near the brokenhearted and saves those who are crushed in spirit", just know that God will help you navigate this heaviness. Peace and joy are in the mist to be the strength, be the light, be the guide and be the joy.

I heard someone say that sometimes grief is the price we pay for love, but it was worth paying. Grief has done become a tattoo on my heart that I proudly wear because it reminds me of my mother's love. Grief sometimes feels like modules that combine together, through unbearable elements. You feel like you're in this cycle of long-suffering that will never end. A lot of time you feel like grief is suffocating you leaving you gasping for air. This is why I learned how not to dwell on the death of my mother but to celebrate her life. I do something that she would have loved at least once a month to help me balance my grief. I started reciting affirmations that help me speak good things into existence. I learned my triggers and how to work through them.

One last thing, your grief isn't the sum total of who you are. Remember to give yourself grace in this season, no matter how many days, weeks, months, or years it may take. You are not your grief. I hope you feel seen, loved, heard and that your grief gets easier after reading this book. Here it is 15 years later, and I am just now able to properly process my grief and put words to my pain. I pray that you find peace in your pieces and give yourself the grace to grieve and grow. Remember, your process is your process. I want to encourage you to silence the outside voices and grieve your way! **You know why? Because you don't have to be the strong one!**

www.ingramcontent.com/pod-product-compliance
Lightning Source LLC
Chambersburg PA
CBHW070942160426
43193CB00011B/1774